A Z-hearted Guide
to Heartache

Charley Barnes

*I hope you enjoy these —
Thank you so much for
the support!*

Barnes

x.

V.

Published in the United Kingdom in 2018

by V. Press,

10 Vernon Grove,

Droitwich,

Worcestershire,

WR9 9LQ.

ISBN: 978-1-9998444-4-8

V.

To Mum, thank you for teaching me to be fine

V.

V.

Contents

V.

V.

My therapist says...

I tell my therapist that I don't want to be
the sort of person who prefixes sentences with:
"My therapist says..."

My therapist says that's an irrational concern.

My therapist tells me that you've told her that I'm writing
on the walls again: hurried hieroglyphics
scribbled around the house. I tell my therapist
how telling the assumption is that if you can't
understand something it must be foreign.
This worsens your ignorance; it doesn't excuse it.

I tell my therapist that when I'm talking to you, I start
sentences with 'My therapist says' to legitimise my claims.
My therapist asks whether I think that's a sensible thing
to be doing to my partner. And I tell my therapist that it is
ambiguous, but also the only way I can get anything done.

When my therapist asks why I'm writing on the walls again,
I tell my therapist in a level tone:
"There are important things that I need to write down."

A pocket-sized guide to hurting yourself

Step One: Fall in love with someone
who doesn't know how to love you back.
Tell yourself that they don't actually lack
the ability to love you, so much as the desire to.
Learn that you are unlovable.

Step Two: Stay with that person.

Step Three: Tell your friends how unloved
you are until you become unliked.
Ask for advice then steadfastly ignore it.
Cry, a lot; if you can cry on the shoulders
of people who don't care, this helps.

Step Four: Start lying to the people closest
to you. You can only get close by pretending
so you must pretend; pretend like you've never
pretended anything before in your life –
pretend you're fine; pretend *this* is fine.

Step Five: Realise that nothing about this is fine.

Congratulations, you have reached isolation!
Your friends and family no longer know how to help;
they no longer want to.
And the person who should care still doesn't.

Step Six: Tell the person, the one who can't
love you, that you might leave.
They will panic, and love you
for a short while; a love harder
than you've ever been loved before.
This will validate your decision to stay with them.

To continue hurting, please return to Step Two.

When buying myself a human

I wish I could unzip his chest, pull apart
his rib cage and take a good look,
like a prospective buyer surveying a new house.
I would flick light switches up, down, up, down, up, down.
It's best to know up front about faults
in the electrics; otherwise, on days like today,
when I flick him on and he stares back blankly,
I'll always assume that it's me, rather than
something that pre-dates my moving in.
I'd ask an independent expert – not his ex –
whether there's rot in the walls, whether
in winter we can retain good heat,
whether he's likely to stop
talking to me on a whim.
I'd invite friends over for a viewing;
friends who've bought their own houses
already, friends who have steady lives
and loves, and I'd say:
"What do you think of the structure?"

    Because we're shallow and we like pretty,
    I'd not mention my fears of subsidence
    or sporadic coldness, regardless
    of the fires lit. His rooms are cramped
    although there's the promise of expansion,
    and he's facing towards the sun now,

but the previous owner warned me
light levels are subject to change...

After talks with my friends, quick chats
with the neighbours, a brief look at his history,
I'd pull the front door closed;
zip his open chest together.
I would call the vendor, name my price,
explain that I've always wanted a long-term project.

Trying too hard

When I was younger trying too hard was a good thing;
being "too helpful" wasn't even a phrase.
I spent my childhood days trying too hard
to stitch trying too hard into my DNA
because trying *this* hard was thought admirable.

But when he, narrow-eyed and sharp-tongued,
tells grown-up me that I'm trying too damn hard,
he hurls the words like hardball insults.
My best quality is now the one that tests him
and his patience the most.

So I peel back skin, pull out parts
of myself and begin to unpick their stitching.
He catches me, shakes his head, laughs, and leaves –
on his way out he tells me how typical it is
that I'm trying too hard. Again.

The first man who broke my heart

He left big shoes to fill;
I stuffed them with mismatched socks.
Pulled shirts from the wardrobe and resisted
the urge to fold them properly.

Books and ring-binders were boxed up,
papers re-shuffled because I couldn't stand
the thought of making his life easier.
I put CDs back in the wrong cases

after running keys, blades, gravel over them.
He made me hate indie-pop-punk of the 90s.
I tried to forget his phone number,
reminded myself that he wouldn't answer anyway.

His spaces were filled with new clothes, bad attitudes,
and men who weren't right for me;
it became something that I looked for –
a clear expiration date.

Twelve months later he came back to explain
different grass was not greener, or easier to love.
Your parents aren't supposed to teach you these lessons,
but at least my dad gave me something of use.

Falling out of love

I thought it would be an epiphany –
I'd wake up one morning and the world would have shifted,
lifted off its axis slightly. I'd swing my legs out of bed, tread
lightly along the floor from our bedroom to our bathroom,
where I'd inspect myself for any physical differences.

But it happened gently.

It happened so that I barely even noticed –
there wasn't a thunderous clap or a series of warnings;
or maybe there was, maybe we just ignored them.
Either way these days I look at him differently, feel him
differently, love him differently. I realise

falling out of love is a slow, but steady, drop.

On trying to not ~~conjure~~ an ex-lover

The lies are so well-rehearsed that they slip
honey-covered into the ears of unsuspecting listeners.
There are still so many days when he's mentioned.
~~But I don't talk about him half as much as I used to.~~

"Did you hear about when Blank and I..."
I censor him; only appropriate after eight at night
and two glasses of wine, by then I'm not saying his name,
I'm chanting it in front of my television,
in the hope that he might manifest post-watershed.
~~Not that I'd care even if he did.~~
Every three times I look over my shoulder
but he is never there – won't be there. ~~He never really was.~~

~~I spend most of my early-twenties uncertain~~
~~of whether I want him to be.~~

Smoking gun

If I had to make you into a metaphor,
you'd be a smoking gun.

In the case of Me versus Everyone, you
are the damning piece of evidence.
You blow everything wide open:
"Look how much I can make her feel!"

You state your case to a jury of my peers
who'd ceased believing I could feel
more than cynicism and scepticism.
I tell you: "They're my basic emotions."

Now the jury is peering into my rib cage,
sitting snug beneath a pock-marked torso.
You spit the most beautiful bullets.
"I don't tend to wear my heart on my sleeve,"

I say, but now it's beating out of my chest.
A Kevlar vest suddenly seems sensible.

Food is an important part of any relationship – Part One

I can't walk past a pizza place without thinking of you.
I wonder what kind of ham they use;
whether you'd be better with a thick-crust margarita.
You always have been a fussy eater,
although you'd wrinkle your nose at me saying that.

Remember when I put parsnip in your root mash?
You acted like I'd trashed your trust in us,
as though you'd never felt more betrayed.
In hindsight, the parsnip may have been a metaphor.
I don't know what for, but that parsnip may one day evolve
into a thousand things we could never bring ourselves to say.

Maybe that parsnip is why our twenty-something-selves
ordered so much damn pizza. Maybe when our pizza delivery
was wrong, it only added credence to the parsnip scenario.
Nowadays I picture our forty-something-selves, fighting
over the same fucking parsnip.
Citing *that* as the moment *this* started to go wrong.

A cure to loneliness

When I tell my next-door neighbour: "Sure, it's nice
to live with someone, but I still get lonely sometimes."
He replies: "I hear you. That's why I use chatrooms."

I want to ask whether his wife knows but the words catch,
suspended on the tip of my tongue while grey matter talks
to grey matter and asks: Should his wife know, do you think?

Thoughts battle it out in the back of my brain, fighting
over modern-day ambiguities while this neighbour tells me
that it's only for company: "Nothing dirty or improper."

I believed him until he mentioned that. Now he's chasing his tongue
down the street, tripping over words that are falling
like rowdy toddlers, desperate to be heard.

I shout over him to explain that: "It still doesn't seem right."
Again he tries to respond and so I click the cross in the top right corner.
I am worried what this conversation means to him.

Pharyngitis

As an on-stage speaker, I'm always looking
for a symbolic meaning when I lose my voice.

Not that I want to believe that my own words
have abandoned me by choice;
rather that they have been plucked from me,
like fleas from a dog. My throat feels
cavernous, the walls rough to touch.

I imagine forceps reaching into my larynx
to pull out a tumour of sounds. Not yet
even heard but nipped in the bud
before someone notices them –
before they can do any real damage.

I wonder whether I've coughed them up,
ball-like, during the night. Whether I slept
with my mouth open too wide
and they tumbled out, lost somewhere in bed,
or were accidentally eaten by the dog.

I know in my gut, where words
are still waiting to be catapulted up,
that it isn't a case of language abandoning me
but life-tiring. One hundred miles an hour
is not a manageable speed long-term –

sometimes, I need the quiet.

Tips to fix a depressed person

Don't
assume that you can do what modern medicine struggles to.
You're not Prozac, or Lexapro, or Paxil;
you're not designed to remedy this imbalance,
but don't assume either that that makes you a cause of it.

Don't
take a depressed person's depression personally,
especially if they're your partner.
Even if you do have a habit for being happy –
depressive grey takes more than being told to smile before it will shift.

Don't
be miserable with them because they're miserable with you
because 1) they aren't miserable with you and 2)
only one of you is making a conscious effort to be miserable
with the other. The other person is actually miserable today.

Don't
confuse their illness with their existence. People *have* depression
much like the author *has* red hair and the reader *may* need glasses.
But as autonomous individuals, we are ultimately more than the sum
of our chemical parts: serotonin does not maketh the (wo)man.

Don't
tell them you wish you could fix; their depression; their brain;
their anything. They're not broken, merely bent,

but even on the days when emotions are pretzel-shaped
and they're bending over backwards to push you further away –
please, take note of this:
they're still not here to be 'fixed'.

Food is an important part of any relationship – Part Two

For the third time in a row you ask for a takeaway,
even though cheat day is Saturday
and I haven't lost a single pound this week.
I shred lettuce leaves and ask for a subject change.

"Have you thought about calling the doctor...

...using your crutches?

What about the wheelchair, just when we're walking far?"

A stray tear tumbles into your salad dressing.
I wish I had ordered Chinese.

The Girl who openly discusses sex in a coffee shop

"I'm pretty sure that some weeks we have sex
because we worry what it will mean if we don't."

The Girl in Starbucks says this unashamedly
to the girl sitting opposite her, and unknowingly
to everyone in a three-table radius. Her friend says:
"But like, isn't that really depressing, for you?"

The Girl says: "A little, but it's hard to be depressed
when you're having an orgasm, right?"
The Woman two tables away from The Girl tuts,
and looks at me. I want to shout but don't.

How cruel: The Girl can't talk to her partner
about problems with sex, so she talks to her friend
about problems with sex, but now strangers have a problem
with her talking about sex, and it's no wonder,

really, that we still lie down and spread our thighs,
wider than a tutting mouth.
It's hard to be oppressed when you're having an orgasm.
Right?

Another cure to loneliness

He's wiping what could be chlorine from his forehead,
expels air hard, and pulls back hard, as if letting the breath
slip out were a mistake.

Our blood-shot eyes lock onto each other, two tables apart,
he says: "I never know when to stop." He laughs,
asks if I always swim here, tells me...

and adds to this sentence until it sounds like a paragraph;
he's right, I think, he doesn't know when to stop.
The words rattle out for so long my hair is nearly dry.

But that's fine, there was a time when no one
was waiting for me at home either.

#AmIPrettyYet

When I upload a selfie, captioned: "feeling a little vain",
what I'm really trying to do is ascertain how many strangers
find me fuckable enough for me to leave the house today.

I hashtag it as many times as socially acceptable, no spaces
between the words so they sit as crushed up as the ego
that drafted them. Depicted on the screen, see hashtag:

#girlswhoread #girlswithglasses #redheadedgirls
#gingergirls   #curlyhairedgirls   #girlswithhair   #girlswithfaces
#girlswhohaveabandonedtheirselfworthinpeculiarplaces

And then I wait for a like. In the bottom right of the screen
the hearts pile up as strangers throw their love at me.
Ten minutes in, I've got double digits; I won't leave the house

for less than three. Seventy-eight strangers tell me that
I look nice today. One comment reads: Daaaayum.
It feels good to know I have distorted the English language

but that passes, replaced by what feels like a physical pain.
Make-up wipes at the ready, I strip my face down again;
discard my clothes; one by one, I cover all mirrors.

In my inbox, there are fifteen new messages to read,
but instead I back-click, delete the image from my feed.
I didn't feel like leaving the house today, anyway.

An apology for not looking disabled

This isn't a poem so much as an apology to anyone
who's ever eyed me suspiciously for using a blue badge,
even though my legs are working. I should pour myself
from my open car door into a mangled mess on the ground,
while yelping for my carer to click my limbs back together.

Strangers, I'm sorry that my disability hasn't announced itself
with disfigured jazz hands. Sorrier still that my legs
are running on automatic, and that my mother no longer
has to manually manipulate me from the driver's seat
of a saloon selected because the boot
was big enough for a wheelchair.

Elders, forgive my disability for wrapping itself around
my central nervous system; forgive it for being broken
down into an acronym that isn't well-known enough
to be considered a mainstream health condition.
I'm of the hipster generation; I need my malfunction
to be something that most doctors don't recognise.

Newcomers, my apologies for not explaining my nerves,
and how they misunderstand stress as physical pain.
How, when I set the time on my badge, I move the dial
with fingers that ache; how, when I stand up from my seat,
I'm on legs that I can't feel. Newcomers, my apologies
for not explaining that my disability isn't your business.

Surplus information

You'll only eat ready salted crisps and, despite
being a grown up, you still can't properly pronounce
certain words: lawnmower; castle; gorilla.

You're at your angriest when playing games,
but also your funniest. The names you call me
are always softened by victory kisses.

You love comedians, podcasts, new information,
and anything that makes you laugh. Anything
that you can share: "An octopus will rip off…"

When given the option of sleeping or waking up,
it will always be sleep.
Unless the thing you're waking up for is pizza.

You use curse words when you're sleeping.
I don't know who needs to fuck off but some nights
I too wish they'd leave us alone.

You love cider, but our fruitless excursions
for *that* particular cider are one of the most frustrating
dates we share as a couple. Still looking though.

I've studied you. Listened to audio recordings
and highlighted your text messages
to extract the most important information.

I can't remember anything from GCSE maths,
but I know you dressed up as Elvis Presley
for your eleventh birthday. I hadn't even met

you then, but somehow I've gathered parts
of your life and stashed them around my own.
I know far too much now for you to ever leave.

Food is an important part of any relationship – Part Three

When I squeeze your hand a fraction tighter than usual,
you know one of two things has happened:
there are pin-prick pains pattering along my legs again,
or those same legs are threatening to give out entirely.
I've convinced myself that a raid of enraged nerves
can be bated by a hand-hold. I shouldn't squeeze,
but we know that it's a formed habit now.

You've always said it doesn't change a thing.
When patches of my body become numb; when my knees are red
from scratching at itches that are under the skin;
when you're holding me steady because I'm still too stubborn
to use walking aids, even when I need them.

You take my medical history in your stride,
but when my knee buckles again for the fourth dip that day,
I wobble, and the garlic bread I'm carrying
wavers on the paper plate,
heroically you reach out – to catch the garlic bread.

You're brave enough to battle a broken nervous system,
but the thought of food wastage has you rushing scared.
Thank you for being there to save my side order.

Definitely not cures to loneliness

When my mother doesn't answer my phone calls, I text friends:
Hi, how are things? The internet informs me
that on average it takes a friend one hour to reply to such a message.

In that hour, I start to read another book that I won't finish;
I check my phone every five and a half minutes,
because I love my friends enough to believe they are above average.

In between checking my inbox, I check my photo-sharing feed
for images of shih tzu puppies that I'll never meet in real life.
In the background, Buffy the Vampire Slayer saves the world

for the seventh time (the thirteenth time I've seen her
do it). As background noise goes, it's one of my most violent
choices, but the cast's voices are comfortably familiar now.

When that first hour has slipped away, I text again,
different friends, as though I can rewind the misspent minutes.
I raid the kitchen, check the washing basket, hover over names

on my computer screen to see whether people are online.
It's nearly midday. I respond to emails asking me to do this,
and that, and the other. I smother myself with workloads

that I invariably struggle to balance. I edit an essay, start writing
another novel, draft a poem, call my mother, leave her a voicemail,
watch a different episode, take the dog outside, ask my sister

about her day. I pin-ball between bedroom and bathroom, upstairs and down, plan dinner and realise that I have forgotten lunch. Thank God, this must mean the clock is moving again.

It all starts with an acorn

A friend's daughter pointed you out to me.
I picked you up and stashed you,
absent-mindedly, in my pocket.
Later I set you to soak. I hoped you wouldn't float,
and felt encouraged when you settled,
surrounded by opalescent bubbles.

I filled a container; drilled holes; collected soil,
and then I buried you, one and a half times
your diameter. You were hiding close enough
to the surface for me to find you
when I needed to. But I left you outside;
close to morning sun and afternoon shade.

"Stand back and wait," said everyone who knew
I'd waited three years already. "Be patient,"
said those who knew you were my fourth attempt.
"But this could be the start of something special!"
"It could be, but it might not be, you know?"
they'd all gently remind me.

Today, you are nearly three feet tall;
small by comparison to some, but the same
size as your human counterpart. Now she collects acorns
by the bag-full, keeps a firm hold of them until home.
She asks me if we should soak the prettiest of them –
I tell her the most unexpected acorns make for oaks.

Dad's poem

Writing about him
makes me feel like I'm cheating
or betraying her.
She'll worry when she reads this,
wonder what the poem means.

It means it's due time
to hold him accountable:
for the fifteen missed birthdays,
three degrees, graduations,
driving lessons and first car...

For all the earthquakes
that we handled, she handled,
without needing him.
It's time now that we tell him:
we did just fine on our own.

The lie my mum told me

I was raised by a warrior – worrier: in our house,
the words came to mean the same thing.
Mum put on her war paint every morning: eye-liner, lipstick,
a moisturiser that made her glow, so no one would know
she'd been up all night worrying about two daughters.
One readying to take exams, the other caged in by metal,
wheels strapped to her thighs. Mum, bright but teary-eyed,
told me the tried and tested lie:
"You have to keep going, don't you?"

V.

Charley Barnes is a Worcester-based poet and author who has recently completed her Doctorate degree in Creative Writing. Her poetry has been published in a number of anthologies, and her debut prose collection, *The Women You Were Warned About,* was published by Black Pear Press in May 2017. Her unconventional speakers are a mix of personal experience and creative licence. *A Z-hearted Guide to Heartache* is her debut poetry pamphlet.

V.